Lust

poems

Lust

poems

To Lis

Lust for life

Diana

Oct 2013

DIANA RAAB

CW Books
P.O. Box 541106
Cincinnati, OH 45254-1106

Portions of this book have been previously published:
"Shivering" in *Hot Summer Nights: A Collection of Erotic Poetry & Prose* (Inner Child Press, 2012). "Saturned" in *Prairie Wolf Press* (Fall, 2012). "Anecdote to Grief" in *Bubble* (Spring, 2013). "Love's Awakening" in *Snail Mail Review* (September, 2013).

Poetry Editor: Kevin Walzer
Business Editor: Lori Jareo
www.readcwbooks.com

ISBN: 9781625490582

LCCN: 2013954430

Dedicated to all those who lust for life

Also by Diana Raab

POETRY

My Muse Undresses Me (chapbook, 2007)

Dear Anaïs: My Life in Poems for You (Plain View Press, 2008)

The Guilt Gene (Plain View Press, 2009)

Listening to Africa (Antrim House, 2012)

ANTHOLOGIES

Writers and Their Notebooks (University of South Carolina Press, 2010)

Writers on the Edge: 22 Writers Speak About Addiction and Dependency edited with James Brown (Modern History Press, 2012)

MEMOIRS

Regina's Closet: Finding My Grandmother's Secret Journal (Beaufort Books, 2007)

Healing With Words: A Writer's Cancer Journey (Love Healing Press, 2010)

SELF- HELP

Getting Pregnant and Staying Pregnant: Overcoming Infertility and Managing Your High Risk Pregnancy (Hunter House, 1999)

Your High Risk Pregnancy: A Practical and Supportive Guide with Errol Norwitz, M.D. (Hunter House, 2009)

Contents

PAINTING   1

SPEAK   2

LUST   3

PICK UP   4

LOVE'S AWAKENING   5

YOUR SPOT   6

OUR INSOMNIA   7

RIP ME   8

THE FIRST TIME   9

YOUR PRESENCE   10

THE VISITOR   11

THE WAVE   12

SHIVERING   13

WHAT WE HIDE   14

WAITING AND WONDERING   15

TALK   16

REMNANTS   17

RECYCLED MEMORIES   18

FROM BEHIND   19

GOING NUTS   20

WHAT WOMEN WANT   21

MUSE ME   22

FOUND   23

SATURNED   24

MY MORPHINE   25

MUSIC TALK   26

LOOK   27

ENLIGHTENMENT   28

ORGASM   30

TWO WORLDS   32

FINGERS   33
MARCH   34
CREATE   35
ONENESS   36
LEASHED   37
DO YOU REMEMBER?   38
FEVER   39
BOUQUET OF ENERGY   40
HOTEL SOUNDS   41
CHIPPED   42
BEFORE WE MEET   44
CLOUDED LOVE   45
ATTACH / DETACH   46
BALCONY   47
EMOTIONAL ROLLERCOASTER   48
COPING   49
MOONS MAZES MAYHEM   50
NEVER   51
ON THE OUTSKIRTS   52
SAFETY   53
PROTECTION   54
SEXLESS   55
SEXUAL REVOLUTION & EVOLUTION   57
CARD GAME   59
I WOKE UP   61
LIGHTNING   62
CENTURY   63
ALONE   64
NO FEAR   65
THANK YOU   66
STOLEN   69

SPRAWLED 70

PHONE HUGS 72

PANIC ATTACKS 73

ANECDOTE TO GRIEF 74

QUESADILLAS 75

FALSE CRAVINGS 76

SEDUCTION 78

VOLUMES 79

YOUNGER MAN AND OLDER WOMAN 80

YOUR EYES 81

TITS 82

ANSWERS 84

YOUR LIGHTNING ROD 85

TIED HANDS 86

A GENTLE REMINDER 87

THE END 88

WHERE ELSE 89

Acknowledgments 91

About the Author 93

PAINTING

From the first moment we met
I painted your body with my long black hair,
wisps up and down from your afro head
to your perfectly aligned toes.

You shivered in delight
and then my finale
was creating an egg-cracking
like sound over your head
trickling its contents
with the light touch
of my fingertips
down your body
until you begged me to stop.

For years on end
that was our tantra,
well at least until our firstborn
erupted and when my hair got cut into
the 'new mom bob' which you detested
because it altered our sexual rituals.

Now decades later,
you paint your own art
on metal canvases crushed
and shellacked, as I sit in this rocking
chair hoping and praying,
you are never able to crush
the heart that has adored you for so long.

SPEAK

Speak to me like the water
that pours from your kitchen spout
an endless stream of molecular words
to release your inner feelings and fears.

Release me from my misery
and let us dance together in your stories
as you slowly remove
every inch of my clothing

which you examine like a child
who holds a glistening stone
on some remote beach as you whisper
your admiration into my perched ear.

Share your desires and haunts
and I will nestle them near my heart
and nurture each syllable while
you enter me, and when you are there

I shall sing the sweet song of joy
and pray for lasting feelings
and that you never leave my moistness
with your unique firmness. Release yourself
into me and I shall clamp your essence shut.

Tell me you've given up so much
for me and I will tell you the same.
Twist your body around mine
like a snake enveloping its prey.

I am yours
and
there is no
other way to grasp this.

LUST

If you know lust like I know lust
you know how it grabs you
in places that feel so good,
in a way that trumps tomorrow.

It snatches and strangles our pasts away
and forges forbidden futures,
while injecting needles of pure pleasure
into any artery receptive to its dose.

The more you get the more you want
as you climb the hill to survival
to the job which pays
the bills and fills your dinner plate.

When not gasping for pleasure,
the door swings open
on your far side of town
where the bores reside

in boxes stacked upon splintered shelves
their parents have created,
as your independent spirit
branches out to seek

life's rare erotic pleasures
found inside the scrotum
and fallopian tubes
of hidden channels of love

buried in blissful tunnels
until the cell phone rings
and snaps you both back into the reality
which you crave to leave

in a giant step back into the
timeless lustful tunnel of pleasure.

PICK UP

it wasn't your offer
or the way you said it.
it wasn't the way you did it
or how it made me feel.
it wasn't the time of day
or the month or the year
or the shape of the moon caressing us
or how the sun rose when you smiled.
it wasn't how the traffic zipped on the freeway
or how you said good-bye
it was just about the way you loved me
and cared enough to ask.

LOVE'S AWAKENING

What began as an urge to have you,
something primal and needy
turned into a wanting to be one with you.

I blossomed at your fingertips,
I lost myself in your wet kisses
the soft and firm way you held me

walking through the parking lot
to our cars, the grasp which told me
you promised to never let go.

I opened myself to you
like a lily when daylight arrives
and closes up when night springs forth.

Behind our closed doors,
your manly motions warmed me,
all your movements of love

and the way you gave me pleasure—
careful strokes about my body
as I became more vulnerable
under your sacred spell.

Like a rhythmic dance
our bodies became a delicious delight
of magic as I watched
your joy meet mine

under the moonlight
we watched
so many more times
in a lifetime we were never able to share.

YOUR SPOT

The sheets are all ruffled
the pillows tossed in every direction
the water sounds from above
the cars on the streets roar
the curtains you pulled
are drawn closed
the bar stool you sat at spins
like my head around this empty room.

The uneaten dinner sits on the desk
as I find myself on your side of the bed—
because I want your smell
to saturate the pores you left vacant.

This pillow beneath my head
which I placed under yours
when you needed it the most,
lies void of your essence—
while gentle reminders of your explosion
litter my mind—the tension release
during your oasis in the midst of me.

OUR INSOMNIA

Drips from me
slithering its way
up and down both sides
of my exhausted body
in ways I do not understand
inside dreams never actualized

while tears drip into bottomless buckets
pondering of pasts
and dreaming of futures
empty of fun to be had
next to divine wanderings
and lonely hearts.

RIP ME

From the darkness which envelops
my soul, from the horrors of my past
and the tentacles that pull me into the future.

Share with me your moments of Buddhist thought
smothering the icicles suspended from my heart.
Take me into you and hold me tight

and promise never to let go of the child
which craves your protection and love
as you save me from all I am afraid of

and desire. Share with me your secrets,
the tasty juices of your manhood,
the rippling waves which engulf you.

Follow me until the end
and inspire my every word,
pull me back to you and never let me go.

THE FIRST TIME

The moment after we met
and seconds after your smile,
beside me on the old cross-country jet,
I knew that inside a dream our bodies
would one day twist around each other.

And I would lose track of where
yours began and mine ended
and so many other things in my life,
such as my beliefs
or even what happened between us.

I would not recount anything,
not a feeling, a touch or a visual
or the voice you used
to toss me on the bed
and remove my over-the-knee boots
worn during our loving act—

All I will remember is a deep sense
of euphoria transcending every part
of my essence, every hair follicle,
missing breast and scar which makes
me what I am and the idea
and how I will never
walk down the same path again.

YOUR PRESENCE

Even when not
in the same room as me
I feel your intense
and powerful presence

whether yards away
or within the fantasies I create

as I wonder what
this all means in real messages
or it is just something

that propels me forward
or will its intensity
dissipate as this morning's fog.

There are so many things
I wonder about
and beg to ask you

but you are so much bigger than me
and your voice heard
across all peaked mountain tops

and I do not dare step on
your perfectly aligned toes

even though all I want to do
is nibble on them.

THE VISITOR

You come in the night
to whisper your kindness

into my sleeping ears,
as you hypnotize me with your eyes,

your voice, and your ways.
You rip me from a seamless sleep,

as you rustle about my rose garden,
put me in a tizzy and suddenly leave.

Your online words
are coated with warm tea

and when you visit
your limp handshake holds

unanswered questions,
while the observer
pulls feelings out of a bucket.

My shyness, confusion, and fear
envelop every inch of me.

THE WAVE

When we are together
my mind holds an image
of two snakes riding
the wave of desire,
wet and noisy undulations
of overt ecstasy
which enters my room
and without warning
or alarm exits like a flash.

I wonder if you feel the same
intensity which ripples
through my aged popping veins
when I feel my heart stop
at the climax of your desire
as you watch me over and over again
at the pinnacle of what I know to be
the best place for ecstasy.

All I can say is thanks for all
you bring both inside and through me.
The bliss of your healing
lives on, in my every day.

SHIVERING

I am shivering and tingling
in the delight of you

your fluid movements
on the strobe-lit dance floor

your seductive eyes
that have stripped me

and drawn me into your power
in this horizontal position,

as my mini skirt creeps
up my legs rubbing the fishnet nylons

I wore because I knew my excitement
would need an escape

from the intensity of your desire.
I want you more

than I have ever wanted anyone
this tizzy makes me dizzy

as I ponder if it is because
you are the toxic forbidden fruit

which fills my heart with no escape
except for the explosion I share with myself

long after you are gone
back to your wife while I fantasize

about us alone once again
twisted on some hotel bed

far from the real worlds we inhabit
creating our own heaven.

WHAT WE HIDE

Whatever we hide
behind our silly smiles
gets swept up
by undulating burps
looking for hidden remains
which linger long after
the joy dissipates
and love gets filled—
the ethers and pages will be hidden
for too many millennia.

This morning I miss your kisses,
the ones you never smothered me with

yesterday.

WAITING AND WONDERING

Tonight you offered me
the temptation of you on a platter
nestled beside my tight jeans,
silky top and stilettos all wrapped
around the body you caressed just days before
inside and out of the barren hotel room we shared
for moments of undeniable bliss.

Your email subject said, 'possibilities,'
enticing me with an offer
for late evening drinks
but then you went into cyber poof
as you schemed your escape
from the woman holding a gun
to your head and chains to your ankles.

You are a man but afraid of the loss
of the stability of happy homes
and warm, love-filled meals.
For but a moment I blossomed
in the thought of holding you
once again so close even for a moment
but for a moment.

Games are not what I play
off the tennis court,
but tonight our relationship became
a cat and mouse activity
as my clothes lay sprawled out in the closet,
embarked by the nudeness you crave.

Where did you go and when will you return
as I sit here on another lonely night
wondering what will become of us
and the days we cannot spend together.
Please tell me you will be back.
I am unsure if I can go on another day

wondering.

TALK

My lips touch with an irritable silence,
holding inside the pain of losing you,
when suddenly something bizarre happens

during our endless lovemaking sessions,
as if a tap opens wide
and I cannot stop muttering nonsensical sounds
in the ears where others have touched.

With you I learned
that a brain could have a sofa
where words rest until they are ready
to get up and dance about the room,

but until then, they linger like drunks
in the bar five floors below our bed.

Before I let you go, please let me tell you
what it's like to have you inside of me,
your hands which so confidently grasp the hips
which undulate beneath you,

as my voice box offers endless mutterings
exposing the bliss locked up in my psyche,
as if you had injected me
with potent truth serum

while I repeatedly muttered
how I cannot be without you,
or how good it feels
or what my fantasies might pull me to you.

Lately you talk less and lay there more quietly,
eyes closed and head rotating to and fro
mouth hung open in the ecstasy
that only I understand.

Thank you for setting me free.

REMNANTS

The day after you left
I sat on the ledge of my desires

and spun an intangible invisible web
suspended around my essence

holding the warmth of your trusted touch,
the moisture of your recycled kisses

entangled in the firmness of your caress
while the rest of the world froze

around the mold of you
beside the phone that stopped ringing,

the birds who stopped chirping,
and the waves that finished undulating—

only moments after
the windows got stuck open

leaving the stale air of your absence
empty without your love.

He who returns never left.

RECYCLED MEMORIES

On the top unused stairs of my life
sits a stack of old images

forming an irregular mountain
which explodes with lava woven

and covered with pictures from my past
as clear as the Mediterranean

while others bear a monotonous
murky film of sludge.

I sit back and wonder

why each day of my life
some memories rise to the surface

like the hot air in a steamy room
and others choke in sadness

smothered by pain and emptiness.
Some things just cannot be explained

even if one writes stories on journal pages
strung across an old love's back.

FROM BEHIND

You have written your name
on the ribbon across my back
hidden under my smooth epidermis,
and pressed against my perked nipples
which drip with passion

when they feel you walk inside of me.
When you take me from behind
you remind me how we were
once both animals,
unprotected and free in some jungle—

hot, sweaty and craving one another
as we sat under the latticed baobab tree
and love juices dripped from excited lips
while you grabbed my waist-length hair,
me groaning and pleading for more.

The ribbon across my back
does not warn *handle with care*
so trust me when I say
how I crave what you
are begging to give me.

GOING NUTS

As soon as I see you
put the hotel key into
the chipped paint door,
my heart races and
dampness fills my private parts
nipples perked to your heavens—
the desire bubbles under
my wrinkled skin as I remember
grandma telling me to always
want sex because it keeps
your heart beating fast
and your essence vibrant
while on the outside
you stand counting the minutes
for the hard-boiled eggs—
munching on almonds, the protein
your doctor said you needed,
but instead, I'd rather be
gulping down the protein
you have produced in my honor
in the midst of all the chaos
engulfing our lives as
we live under the same roof, apart.

WHAT WOMEN WANT

The night we sat on the stools
inside the bar in your home town,
you stopped, took a deep breath
and asked what women want,
and then quickly rephrased it
to ask what I want in a man.

I had never been asked this,
so I gasped my own breath,
stared deep into your eyes
and the first thing I said
was love. I need a lot of love.

I need the love my mother never gave me.
I need the love my father took
with him to his grave.

I need everything you want to give me.
I do not need diamonds, designer shoes,
or fancy cars. I do not need
three-story homes or feng shui decorated rooms
or dripping fountains in landscaped
backyards. I do not need vineyards
or private jets. I do not need face-lifts
and tummy tucks.

But what I need is you…
your love and an espresso machine
all wrapped with a blue bow.

Can you give me that for a night?
I will be forever grateful.

MUSE ME

The way you look at me,
love me, hold me and kiss me
wants me to pour endless words
into empty pages from here until eternity.

Being wisped away by your passions
and make me yearn
to count the stars
between here and there

and walk the highest of mountains
and swim the widest of oceans
all in response
to that very special moment

when your eyes link with mine
in the deepest night on the quietest
and longest day of the year
that we spend together
in each other's arms

FOUND

The day my first story came to me
I started smelling roses around you
and suffocated in my own delight.

Friends do not meet one another
they knew each another
from the very beginning…

SATURNED

Your planet encircles mine
Once a year
when you call
to the phone I once held
and which now sits
in the dark at the back
of my old underwear drawer
in the empty bedroom
where you stayed
on that night you whispered
how I was no longer the fantasy
of all your unmet dreams.

MY MORPHINE

Seeing you, touching you, kissing you
is the morphine which I love and hate.

It is the cure for the wounds
anchored in my psyche,

this confusing package
I inhabit.

When you are far away,
being without you comes easy

but like morphine, the more I lay my eyes
on you, the more I want, need, and crave you.

One might say that one day
my addiction may just kill me,

but, my hope is you shall never
use this power against me

or that like an overdose,
I shall spasmodically fall to the ground

in a place distant from the warmth of your
caressing and welcoming arms.

MUSIC TALK

There is something about
the sounds of music
ringing in the ears during love making
which meets the rhythm
of a lover's movements in final climax.

LOOK

Your eyes tell it all
love seesawing back and forth

between desire and forbidden territory
as confusion lingers still, this many

years later, when you hold me in your arms
and wonder why the huntress

has this controllable sense that being
in your presence is all I want

and even though
I have my life and you yours

we will meet at the end
of some road, maybe

in this life and maybe not,
these answers are unbeknownst to me

and in many ways I prefer it that way.
May peace fall on your stars.

ENLIGHTENMENT

When you lay there
your jeans, striped blue sweater,
and slim black belt tight about your trim waist,

you asked me what I promised to give you
as you thrust your head back
in the fantasy of our bliss yet to come.

I realize that you, the giver wants
to once in a while be taken
and allowed to become submissive

at the hands of a woman's passion,
so piece by piece I remove
one sock, one pant leg

and handmade sweater
covering your green tee.
Under the touch of my spell,

you writhe in delight,
head tossed upon the fluffy white pillow
as I go down to get my fix

of your manhood
as I shiver in delight
at this place I now call home.

When all of a sudden,
the European part of you,
turns to seize control
and gently rolls me over

to have your six foot way with me.
For the next five hours
we roll around and I ponder how

I never understood where enlightenment
was born, but now I see
it comes from the magic
and the joy of mutual passions

when two bodies become one,
under the whitest of sheets.

ORGASM

You have never really told me
which ones are the best
or which you would
rather do without.

Writhing, restless, and begging
for more, you arrive
just as eagerly on lonely nights
as you do on spontaneous love trysts.

You possess me
and borrow from me
until we get interrupted
by foreign night sounds

or annoying phone calls
which force us have to
stop and start all over again.

Sometimes I think life
is centered around you—
like the lion of the zodiac
always reaching for the pedestal

or the joystick which brings
you towards me, so warm, so firm,
so friendly in the darkness which hides
surgical flaws and yellowing undies

stolen by time
and sent to me in the night
by you, the one I love
and want to spasm with

over and over again.
Thinking of you
or anything connected with you
creates joyous contractions
in places saved only for you.

TWO WORLDS

Let's live in two worlds
the way lovers do
the way we should
the one we face every day,
littered with family goings on
and work affairs and then
let me gently meander over to your world
the world of great imaginations,
travels to untouched venues
sleeping in beds never opened
holding hands in foreign streets
walking new mountains
tasting sweet foreign foods
all while gazing into those
deep brown bedroom tunnels
which always tell me they want me,
sometimes slits, sometimes
wide open in amazement
at the pleasures
my lips bring to yours.

Where did you come from
and please don't tell me
that you will ever go.

Promise?

FINGERS

I feel your fingers
touching every part
of my psychic being
rummaging around
my cells performing
surgical acts of kindness
trying to figure out
reasons for being
and then moving on.

MARCH

The ides of March
walk their way
between pillars of love
icicles on hot body parts

as you march to and fro
following paths
where we cannot go
desires enter into soft nights

but sometimes hammers
upon softened heads
and footsteps which
move between tiptoed desires.

Simple wants turn into
complicated lifestyles
rampant emotions echoed
through tunnels of love

that once were
left with no voices to hear
how we want to be alone
inside a cocoon.

Where resides the real moment
we need and desire?

Dreams that live empty lives
until you walk over
place your hand calmly into mine
and whisper

it will be okay—
please trust
please don't die
please have no fear.

CREATE

Make me the person I want to become

draw from me the secrets buried under

the façade of responsibilities.

Allow me to be who I want

as I whisper secrets into the pockets

of your open mind and the doorways

to your heart. Make me the one

you wake to every morning,

the coffee that brews you, the ice cream

which smothers you. Steal my heart

and hold it with your sculpted muscles,

massage it as if you want to keep it forever

and most important, please don't tell

anyone our little secret of the person

we will become together.

ONENESS

When we lie together
me on your barely shaven chest
your legs snaked around mine,
I feel this intense sense
of oneness, a merging
of sensibilities, cultures
sensualities and adoration
woven into the ethers we share
with the ambient air.

One can get lost
in this sense of euphoria
this after-sex delight
when everything seems right
and we are so very tight
within the provided boundaries
submerged in the realities of cannot
when I turn to you
in that window of ten minutes
to ask if you love me.

When you kiss my forehead
squeeze my deltoids
and say that
is a rhetorical question
anything else you want to know.
You say I have eight more minutes
and my time is ticking
and so is this big heart for you.

LEASHED

She has put you,
my master, on a short leash
but it really should be

the other way around
me on the leash as you
hold me between

the space in your two front teeth
beside your rapidly rotating tongue
bringing euphoric bliss

to each female part of me.
If you were on my leash
it would look like you ordering me

where to go and what to do
who to kiss and who to miss.
By now, you should know,

how much I prefer when
you are the one in charge.

DO YOU REMEMBER?

Do you remember
as clearly as me
and yesterday's star
the moment our eyes
linked on that beach
in the midst of heaven
when we realized
where we were
supposed to be
and every soldier was
in his proper place
and every shoe lined
up in the closet of time
and every crystal
and kernel of sand
glistened under
its new quarter moon
where you felt you could
walk on water
without being called God
and offer hope to
anyone needing it
all because she walked
into your life and emptied it?

FEVER

You arrive in my arms
on that deep full moon night
shivering sheepishly, and I ask about

that fever and if it is
because you have not seen me
in more than two weeks—
or if it is the seeing me
or the fear of being discovered
by hidden entities

or

do you feel sometimes like a bad boy
is that why you shiver?

I feel like an enabler
but I really do not care
all I want is you
as much as I never want you to know.

BOUQUET OF ENERGY

When you enter me
there is this indescribable
surge of emotions
and tingles rummaging
through my aged body,
your designer cologne
dripping into all
the crevices you visit
and a bouquet of sex exudes
into the perimeters
of the room
we will soon call our own.

I am at that moment
an indescribable spirit,
a bird in the sky
a fish in the water,
an animal roaming
unknown forests
touching foreign parts
feeling quite familiar
in this oasis we have
created for one another.
Our very own place
untouched by anyone
or anything ever before.

HOTEL SOUNDS

This place so far from home
usually screams quiet
but on the day we met
the neighbors' noises
almost disturbed those
emanating from our room.

When you pressed those pillows
on top of my face
to hide my exploding joy
in the everlasting eros
you invited me into you
on the very day
you ordered our double espressos
and your alias Jay
during the beautiful month of May.

The moment I whispered eternity
you looked at me
and your eyes said it all
as your heart pulled back
afraid to chase me away.

CHIPPED

Today when you landed your tired body
heavily into my arms
you warned me that life has chipped

away at the crystals which made
you the wonder you are,
and that the love buried in your heart

might have to lay dormant
until all of life's horrors evaporate
into the darkest clouds
suspended each day above your head.

Now, beside me is the fluffed pillow
where you nestled your head,
now empty and grasping

like a warm spoon of melted chocolate
sinking into my hungry mouth,
and where you nudged and pushed yourself
deeper into my heart.

Right now all I want to do is stay here
in the same position we were in together
only moments earlier
until my sun sets in its sky forever.

I have waited so long for this moment
and the weeks have blurred in
to one another
chugging along like winding roads

in an obscure desert, sometimes
meandering for indefinable days.
Really all I want to do is cast my fishing

rod out into the universe and save you
from all that irks you while whispering
in your ear how I never want you to leave,
the spell you say I have cast.

Fantasies are like that.

BEFORE WE MEET

I get this burst of enthusiasm

this oozing sensual adrenaline
excitement, thrills and appetites whet—

my palpitations become inaudible
and my nervous system searches

for a break in the firing of neurons
then I turn around to see your arrival
before my eyes
and during the next few hours

it all passes in slow motion
as I watch your every move

and listen to each whisper
and then without warning

your visit evaporates
like the steam from my kettle

into an untouchable air.
I turn around and wonder

if your visit was merely
a dream and then the phone rings

silence ensues
and normalcy follows suit.

CLOUDED LOVE

Rushing through the clouds
with white wings
my mind wanders to me
cuddled in your arms
trying to figure out
when the back of my head
will be pierced by your love
trembling in this crystalline heart
you left on my bedside table
falling to the ground on the day
you packed your bag
and hers hidden in the back drawer
of your mind
to head to the valley of the love
which dissipated
like the vapor of the clouds
I roll through right now—
this many miles above the love
I thought I once had.

ATTACH / DETACH

What is it about
this idea of holding on
to what we cannot have
the enticement and adoration
the tips of our claws
which grasp and do not let go
whether it is a lover or a pair of shoes.

Our fears are mirrors
and our essence lies on tables
of doctors' offices
sharing fantasies
of love gone by.

BALCONY

You walked me to that balcony
always a very sacred place for me

maybe going back to Romeo and Juliet
and the romances buried in the heart.

The point is, I could not believe
the intense flutterings inside my own organ

when you leaned me against the railing
ten feet up from waterlogged swans

which pierce their eyes into the back of my head
as you told me you wanted me

like you never wanted anyone before
but that you would wait

for the time to be right.
I blushed and sighed

and pushed your manhood into me
fantasizing of the wonder

and how long could I hold out
before deciding the best thing

to do is to toss you into the waters
which will eternally hold our fate.

EMOTIONAL ROLLERCOASTER

My psyche lately
has been akin to an
emotional rollercoaster
slithering between the hills and valleys
over mountain ranges
and low flying planes
while my fingertips
barely hold on
to these flooded emotions.

I feel my slow
wet and slippery slippage
from the grime
dipped into at the beginning of each day
my craving for freedom
beside the pain which burrows
its hole in this horny heart
sometimes made of steel,
other times a child's pliable clay.

COPING

People ask
how does one cope
when your loved one clicks their heels
and decides to walk out the door
for some old fashioned sex
with a stranger yet to be met,
and what I tell them is
I create my own
affair between me and my computer
composing descriptive erotic words
of my last time with someone
who wanted me
in every sense
of the six-letter word.

MOONS MAZES MAYHEM

So it seems to me
there is no other way to see
where shall there be a tree
in your heart.
I will find a key
say you love
all that I do
what I say or who I may be.

Climb Machu Picchu
under our stars
by all its bars
find me a kitchen
to cook it all for you.

Now.

NEVER

You said you have never
had a lover like me
yet when I pushed
you and your manhood
into the bed's corner
to deeply explain, you said
it is complicated
like the climax, relax, and climax
way we make love.

You told me you loved my rhythm
and the way I moved for you
and how I knew you
and how good it felt
inside my darkness
caresses to parts
never touched before
as you wiggle beneath
the body I carve for you
each day in the gym
as the sun rises in its horizon
and the stars twinkle
because you are near me.

I never want to leave here.
I call it infatuation
you say it's love
but who really knows

maybe someone will raise their right hand
to give us the truth we crave.

ON THE OUTSKIRTS

On the outskirts of my mind
your passion whimpers
as fingers grab and hold me down
in the deepest of the night. On the back
of the shoulder which rests upon yours,
there are silhouettes of bodies ripped
apart by heartbreak and places of putty
where you put it together again to make
me the whole I always wanted to be.

Sleeping in your arms I wear the skirt
you have put your hands up once more
in the very short time of our sacred acquaintance.

SAFETY

When I meet someone
for the very first time
I take a quick glance at their hands
which offer glimpses
into their goodness.

Hands and faces protect me
and as strong as I appear,
I seek protection.

When I first saw your hands
on your mother's kitchen table
I had this feeling of safety and protection
in the way I felt protected
in the parking lot when
you walked me to my car.

Safe.

I felt it right away.
It is important.
Feeling safe with you.

PROTECTION

I love how you protect me
from the dangers of myself
for the harm I might inflict
if left alone full of knifed words

on the end of that phone line
digging daggers
into already broken hearts.
From the first day we met
I asked for protection

from childhood dreams
buried in my psyche
never allowed to surface.
As time flowed between us

I noticed that the protection
you really wanted to offer
was the type to guard
me from the rest of the world
stealing me from you.

SEXLESS

The wine glass full
beside its empty bottle,
the dog walked and happy
the microwave beeping
with tonight's dinner delight,
frozen meals to temper
a frigid sensibility.

The empty stairwell
which leads to the barren bed
covered with past passions,
the nightgown once seduced
lies in the bottom drawer
beside the garter belt
bought in a fun frenzy.

I slip into your nightshirt to remind me
of your soft touch and how the tingles
stuck to my skin like honey to the bottom
of a coffee cup. I step into this empty bed,
dog cuddled at its feet to hear
the silent sounds of love gone.

I feel alone in a world of my own doing
and glance at the distant balcony—
but my courage is too short.
I peel the sheets off my squeaky clean body,
and stare at the clock as a reminder
of our passionate lovemaking.
I slowly slip my fingers

into the wettest part of me,

the woman I love to be.
For the first time, I notice
a dryness in the place that once dripped
with desire as I force myself to pleasure.

Against all rationale
I let it happen slowly,
fantasies abound ripping at me
but realize what I really need
is another glass of wine to drown
the sorrows of my privates
and all that resides between deafened ears.

SEXUAL REVOLUTION & EVOLUTION

When I was young and desirable
I looked to you for enlightenment
for freedom from my obsessions
with sensuality and sexuality.

But now sunk into my middle age,
the pulse from my memories
sustains like the morning coffee you served
as I rolled over to see

the smile on your morning face
and am reminded about how you
used to always wake up hard
inside of me first thing in the morning.

Out of my eye's corner
on your wooden night table
there sits a little blue pill
which executes its magic

of blissful journeys accompanied by runny noses
and transports back to forgotten youths
of reading erotic poems
and glimpsing bad pornography.

This seems to be the only way
when there are no other offerings
other than your tight jeans
which remind me

of all that once was
beside my leather mini skirt
which you ever so slowly lifted
when our kids were small and time scarce

as I stood over gas stoves
stirring simmering soups
rocking baby carriages in one hand
and spoon in another, hands tied
and submissive, just the way you

liked me and just the way I wish it were now.
What a way to touch enlightenment.

CARD GAME

From the age of seven
when I counted really well
my grandmother taught me
to play cards, something she
did for extra money each Friday night
at the Buxbaum's apartment on main street.

The first game she taught me
gin rummy—eight card first and then ten,
open-handed and then closed for the big points.

Grandma was unbeatable.
She knew how to place each card
in its right place—suits matching
her favorite red lipstick
painted on using a fine brush
to give a distinguished point
on the top of her lips—any
exaggeration would have made
her look like a clown—an identity
that in no way fit her vivacious
and sexy personality with fawning men
gathered around her in those dance halls
when she met grandpa.

When grandma took her life
as a result of childhood trauma
bubbling to the surface as it sometimes
does when the grays kick in—my mother
decided to use cards as a way
to predict her own future
as if she lacked the insight
to figure it out herself—the third
card dealt would point to her state of mind,
spade meant sad, heart meant happy.

And when this was not enough,
the fortune teller arrived
to the table with her tiny tarots.

Once I never believed
in that cryptic art
but now as life circles back
to the habits of childhood,
I also reach for those
Goddess Guidance oracle cards
to predict who might
want me today under
the largest moon known to
humankind and whether
submissiveness or aggression
is written in the sky.

I WOKE UP

I woke up to a dream that you were in a place

you should not have been and I because of it,

I hurt myself in a way that I shouldn't have.

Some thoughts are better kept to ourselves.

LIGHTNING

when your car pulled up
beside mine in that private parking lot

behind the chocolate shop
with drips of your sweetness,

it wasn't the angle you parked at
or the sparkle in your eyes

or the black shirt slung
down across your privates

or the way your hair slicked back
or the smile reflected

off your car window,
it was the way you opened

the car door to greet me,
your hand suspended

towards me like a
server who offered a yummy

glass of wine,
as you gently elevated me into your arms

while I tottered
on those very high heels

you begged me to wear.
It was the lightning which struck

my heart with the rod of your kindness.
I have never felt like such a woman.

CENTURY

Yesterday when looking
forward into your future
and its past icicles
bottled up in your brain
it felt as if centuries of words
unleashed from your veins
tiny particles exploding
into gigantic revelations
which released you
from the bonds
tied to your new age
of release
like the old oak tree
begging for a friend
to grow old with
as if leaf by leaf
the future was made
and the past made its potent mark
beside ice cream cones
dripping themselves
onto a fertile ground
and a new seed growing.

ALONE

So here I am alone in my bed again. He sleeps in the room downstairs. He says he likes being alone. Is this really true? He used to be easy to read. No more. Those days are done. I no longer know what he is thinking and this aggravates me—he flips all the time—one day this and one day that. Leaving me very confused. I turn over to sleep like the baby I once was and decide....

Life is frustrating, confusing and depressing.

NO FEAR

Go ahead
tell me I have another cancer
say that I only have months to live
or limited sexual encounters.

Tell me what you want to tell me
tell it deep into my deafened ear
and I will turn and walk away
and never believe a word you say again.

THANK YOU

Yesterday, we stood there
near that foreign hotel bed,
your orchid reaching for mine,
tentacles spreading across our miles
while your deep brown eyes touched
inside my green ones,
you gently asked
about a shower encounter.

My eyelashes fluttered in fear,
fumbling for words
as I told you
it would be a first—
a man viewing
my scarred landscape—
ten or more years hence.

'Another first' you ask
and I reply 'what was the other'
and you respond, 'you know,' as you
take my hand sprawled like
a bird drying her wings,
on that soft mattress, you lifting me
onto your shoulder with infantile steps

parading me across
the mercantile carpet
to the pink tiled bathroom
and asking if we should leave
the lights off, as I stare
again into your warm eyes

which tell me how you
want everything to shine on me.

I tell you it is okay for the lights to be on
as my teeth chatter
with fear that you will walk
away in horror of my unevenness
which you have already discovered
under those crisp white sheets,
my loss of purity and beauty,
but to my delight and own shock

you step over the tub's edge
still grasping my hand in yours
to adjust the hot water—as hot
as my body is for you
and the heat feels as if it will burn
my crooked toes but I don't complain,
I have become

the slave I promised to you,
standing face to face while you
make manly adjustments for us—
while a hot stream of water
forms a pocket between our chests
and I focus on that and not
on my lopsided breasts
as I snatch a glance at your
brown seductive eyes—
doing just the same.

You grab a bar of soap
and lather my body, still
staring deeply into my orbits,
lathering me head to toe
and if a woman could have an erection,
then I must have just had my first
right there in the hotel shower
before you laugh and ask
to play 'drop the soap,' and you
have me bend down without trying
anything. Your warm welcoming
words make me wonder where you came
from and all I can do is blush as you beg
me to stay and continue to make me
feel so comfortable with
all I am left with and all
I can muster from my mouth
is thank you and thank you again.

STOLEN

I thought when I saw you
before we entered the dance hall
that someone would steal you away
grab you, sweep you towards them
and you would leave me, standing alone
and come fetch me at the end of the night

but

then I realized that it was me you wanted
slung across your arm facing you
undulating movements back and forth
to the rhythm of soul music
and no other woman mattered
it was just me
at that moment
for however long it might last
I would savor and cherish
the warmth of your caress
the firmness of your body
and the gentleness of your
arm around the waist
I worked so hard to keep small
for you and me.

Thank you for taking me dancing
on your birthday.

SPRAWLED

Moments after we made love,
        transcendence in invisible universes,
                you rolled over onto your stomach

head at foot of bed beside me,
        sheets all confused in their ecstasy
                you in your watery world have gone astray.

You place your chin into your hands
        and stare across the thin-aired room,
                and in my blissful stupor, I imagine

you lying on your ocean wave
        after you just conquered another masterful swell.
                I shake my thoughts to the present

and see you at my side with the energy
        you have taken and given me at the same time.
                I am in awe of these sensations, the tingles

and the joy just passed from your body to mine
        like an octopus' tentacles reaching into my core
                as I turn slightly to glance at your beaming face,

the expression of success for bringing me this much joy
        like the joy your surfboard bestows on you
                without less measure of warmth.

You pull me towards you, your surfboard for the night to lose,
        turn me over and spoon from behind,
                holding me like a loving mother, my silicones
                nestled in your hand

as you dream of flying back to those moments,
 your own mother who battered your psyche
  beside siblings gone for no reason. I remain still

in the pleasure of knowing
 it is me who can help bring you back
  to the sacred memories of your youth

in the same way that you bring this old woman
 back to her own.
  I love the feelings you bring out in me.

PHONE HUGS

Yesterday I needed your phone hugs,
warm words to squeeze my insides
whispering wonderful musings
and cravings upon this lonely heart.

How do we find a balance
in this secretive world
we have created for ourselves,
where freedom is hidden
in the closets we disowned.

How do we get what we
desire without hurting loved ones,
I ask as I glance at the Buddha
on my desk who tells me

like you often have
not to worry, be in the moment
and it shall work out—
be patient, breathe and remember
whatever you do is wonderful!

PANIC ATTACKS

Once every couple of months
someone says something
that sends me into a glob
of quivering of nerves
and then, as if the Kansas tornadoes
had just arrived, I am swept off my feet,
yanked away into a strange yet familiar
land where nothing makes sense
not even the well-meaning remarks
of loved ones or licks from four-legged animals.

My fifth sense speaks whispers that my love
has been between the ears of another woman—
something about the way he says hello,
or how he slams the front door,
coupled with the quick,
dry kiss onto my receiving lips
and the up-to-trouble smirk showing
someone has fiddled with him
or tickled the soft spots I've grown
to adore for the past three decades.

You should know I am a writer,
with an immense imagination,
and if by chance I fabricate such an
encounter, then there's really
nothing to do but to take him back
into my arms. I pull open our front door,
escort him in, my negligee
barely hugging my shoulders,
sheer readiness for our favorite pastime
behind our bedroom door and where
love sounds send waves across our mountains.

ANECDOTE TO GRIEF

Who do you call
who do you run to
when grief knocks
on your back door
when you isolate yourself
from all that is divine,
personal and attached.

Do you reach for the pen
the sex object or the bottle,
the doorknob to heaven
or the syringe…
where do you find
your relief from grief?

QUESADILLAS

remind me of you
because whenever we are out
that is what you always order
if it is on the menu and then
I need to share with you
because that's what we do
share everything
just like two lovers should.
it is bliss.

every minute of it.

FALSE CRAVINGS

Why do we crave what we do not have
why does desire pull strings
of hearts already broken
where do you go when it hurts
where do you go to hide
spreading wings but fear of flights?

Where do the answers lie
but in the crevices of our minds
transcending in universes gone forever
abandoned by cathartic dreams
and lonely nights
left to hugging pillows
and looking into the eyes of furry creatures
who unlike us only want food and love?

Like a bird hovering
over a universe he will never have.
Why does pain make
holes in souls never understood?

Can we put our money
into banks of love
and in hearts where it multiplies
as we clap our hands
after endless paradises of joy
and gutters filled with crap
into corners of empty souls?

Where will these empty pocketbooks
of desire find their solace
if not upon broken doorknobs
never allowed to enter
paths never walked upon?

What is it you do not understand
about the life you created and nurtured
through good and bad
sickness and health?

Where is my respite
or does my resentment resonate
on the edge of my fingertips
barely holding on to a life given to me
on a silver coated platter
that now peels at its edges—
repairs no longer available?

Where are the wounded healers
to show us how to get up off
our scraped knees
and face the world
which looks so very empty now?

Is it too late to patch the tear in the tire
which you rode your entire life?

How can one sing the songs of youth
and roll in the joy we crave?

Is poetry the answer
to who we are and
what we will become
in this life of love gone astray?

SEDUCTION

You never said a word
you never made a nuanced gesture
or took my hand
to tell me you wanted me
you never wrote me a love letter
or said you couldn't wait
until we met again.

You never bought me a present
or said you never met
anyone like me
or that you will miss me
during your month-long travel
or that you knew one day
our paths would cross again.

But today
you could not put your finger on it,
there were so many things you
knew without really telling me
but I knew all the mutterings of your heart
because I could feel the pulses through
the deep look into my green eyes
and the way you seduced
the dormant woman
who had been living dead inside of me.

VOLUMES

If only I could hold for you
the volumes of hair which roll
down my shoulders and neck—
each strand which stole your heart
on its first glance, glistening wisps,
each one to grasp a tentacle of thought
infused with kisses set just for you
and tossed in your direction.

You will wonder what hit you
as I stagger down my spine's stairwell
in search of the crevice which will hide
our secrets like baby bunnies in our garden
hunting for the one who taught him
all he knows, before he starts his love pattern
of babies and passion in the same way
that the volumes of my hair remind you
of all that you gained in such a short time.

YOUNGER MAN AND OLDER WOMAN

My mind is busy touching you
in places you've never been touched
as you are too young to understand
the desires of an older woman who
yearns for young flesh, responsive
parts wanting every part of her
during every breathing moment—
I cannot be patient glancing
at your muscles, the ones sculpted
from the waves which engulf you—
tell me you want me and I promise
to give you everything you need
whenever you want and even
if I need to be on the moon
to pick up a dozen eggs
or the pharmacy to fetch protection
plastic sheaths which will only
bring us that much closer.

YOUR EYES

Always wanted green ones
piercing olives that cast daggers
into lonely hearts,
but nature never lets us have our way
or maybe in passing
they are the ones offering delight
but tonight
your brown eyes offer
what no others
have ever given me,
for a moment or a day—
the pleasures no one
can ever take away
those special moments between us
in the darkness which never ends.

TITS

Your passion for art yanks you
to a photo of a woman's essence—
nurturing round and plump breasts,

similar to the ones which leaked
the very first drop of milk
into your newborn mouth

and nine subsequent months
of maternal attachment.
This morning, I glance down

at my own mammaries, transformed
at the hands of a scalpel, replaced
by earth's salt, as I wonder

if your impulse to paint them
was the mere hunt
for a more perfect pair,
as I undeniably battle

with the loss of what made me
the woman you fell for so many years ago
on that high-grassed hill

beside your parents' farm, above the lake
and around the corner from the rose field
where you got on your knees and gave

me a rosebud and whispered—'this is a bud for a buddy'
as my young heart dropped to your kindness
into the fertile soil beneath my feet

and has remained there
this many years later
succumbed by your adoration.

ANSWERS

I look upon the bark
of a tree suspended
in a yard I never walked
hoping to find you wandering
the same path lost to me
when I bump into your psyche
and you ask for my name
and we scribble something
undecipherable because
what we are called
is of no essence
in the land of sexual fantasies
as someone shouts out
the answer I want to hear.

You tell me to write
and figure out what sleeps
in my broken heart
as though my pen connects
the essence of my secrets
told to everyone but you,
but because my heart bled
on the table where
your wine was served
the one you promised me
for centuries, before I tossed
my sheer clothes to the
shadows of my mind
behind the fires of life—
afraid to leave behind
all that you have given me.

YOUR LIGHTNING ROD

What was in the letter you sent
that item sticking out
from the corners of licked closures,
the bent part of you no one sees
not even me into that
forbidden territory
where foreigners bury
the customs of their youths
and old men pray
that the calendars received
for Christmas' past erase
the years that follow and
that you move the clock hands faster
as I jump rocks before the ocean
you swam miles and miles
of saturated dendrites
squashed between all the
thoughts of me you never
had until our eyes linked
in that far away place
rare people wander
which felt like decades ago
but can you believe
it was only a fortnight ago
you, my fantasy lover.

TIED HANDS

Somewhere between
my half-removed chest
and the two-mile scar on my back
are my left and right arms
tied behind my back
taken prisoner to the times
and elements of these moments
when pain digs its ugly claws
into my heart making some parts
sticky and gooey and the string
holding it together out of what
some might call obligation
and others domination and whenever
I turn, I feel locked up in a cocoon
of torture wondering what it might
take to be set free and capture
more opportunities of all that I want.

A GENTLE REMINDER

On the top shelf
of my second hidden closet
behind the door

where the extra blankets
are stowed, is the secret spot
where your olive green sweatshirt lives

saturated with your sensuous scent.
This piece of clothing
you intentionally

left behind to embed in me
daily vapors of you
but now the scent dissipates

like each day left behind
as the memories of my past
sit under some molten rock,

and dreams of riding the waves
of untouched blissful moments
between transpersonal psyches

amidst giggles masking indefinable tensions
written on the blank walls
of a history which badly needs to be written.

THE END

How is it that a premonition
slips under the layers of my tentacles
waving a signal that tomorrow

is the end of something
which I do not know,
while I try to whisper

and grasp my desires
as temptation tries to whisk
me from the moment.

I cannot, because
one more slippage of disaster
will send me six feet under
without ever tasting the sweet
juice of change and the
euphoria of saying good-bye.

I am sorry.

WHERE ELSE

where else but in art

can you let your fantasies blossom

and dreams flower—

nowhere.

Acknowledgments

My deepest gratitude to all those whose love and support have inspired and encouraged me to launch this book, including my muse Anaïs Nin. Mention of all the generosity goes beyond the profile of this book, however, I would like to express heartfelt thanks to the following for our tête-a-têtes, and musings over coffee or spirits:

Robert Bosnak, Charlotte Rains Dixon, Perie Longo, Marcia Meier, Sena Jeter Naslund, Kim Stafford, David Starkey, Gail and Thomas Steinbeck, Chryss Yost, and to my dearest first readers: Amy Ferris, Molly Fisk, Barry Spacks, Tristine Rainer, and Tony Trigilio.

Heartfelt thanks to Tyson Cornell, Alice Marsh-Elmer, Julia Calahan, Maggie Lang, and Ann Weinstock for your contributions towards the book's editorial and technical aspects. Notable acknowledgment to Kevin Waltzer of CW Books for believing in this project.

And last, but never least, without the unrelenting loving support of my family this book would not have been brought to fruition. Thank you to my beautiful and adoring children, Rachel Miriam, Regine Anna, Joshua Samuel, and son-in-law, Daniel Del Valle. Thank you for being yourselves and for your own creativity, which fires my own. Most of all, merci à l'amour de ma vie, Simon, merci beaucoup pour tout. Je t'embrasse maintenant et toujours.

ABOUT THE AUTHOR

Diana Raab is an award-winning poet, memoirist, and believer in the healing power of the written word. She began crafting poems at the age of ten when her mother gave her her first Khalil Gibran journal to help her cope with her grandmother's suicide. Some years later she discovered the journals of diarist Anaïs Nin and learned that, like Raab, Nin began journaling as a result of loss (the loss of her father). Much of Raab's poetry has been inspired by Anaïs Nin's life and works.

She is the author of four poetry collections, *My Muse Undresses Me* (2007); *Dear Anaïs: My Life in Poems for You* (2008); *The Guilt Gene* (2009); and *Listening to Africa* (2011).

Her poetry and prose have appeared in numerous journals and anthologies including *Rattle, Boiler Room Journal, Rosebud, Litchfield Review, Tonopah Review, South Florida Arts Journal, Prairie Wolf Press, The Citron Review, Writers' Journal, Common Ground Review, A Café in Space, The Toronto Quarterly, Snail Mail Review, New Mirage Journal,* and *Jet Fuel Review.*

She is editor of two anthologies, *Writers and Their Notebooks* (2010) and *Writers on the Edge* (2012), co-edited with James Brown. Both these collections include submissions from poets and prose writers.

She has two memoirs, *Regina's Closet: Finding My Grandmother's Secret Journal* (winner of the 2009 Mom's Choice Award for Adult Nonfiction and the National Indie Excellence Award for Memoir), and *Healing With Words: A Writer's Cancer Journey* (winner of the 2011 Mom's Choice Award for Adult Nonfiction).

Raab is a regular blogger for *The Huffington Post* and writes a monthly column for the *Santa Barbara Sentinel,* "The Mindful Word." She lives in Southern California with her husband and maltese poodle, Spunky. She has three grown children. Raab is currently working on her doctorate in psychology and is researching the healing power of writing and creativity.

CPSIA information can be obtained at www.ICGtesting.com
Printed in the USA
LVOW06s0515070114

368405LV00002B/5/P